Dog Days

YOUR FURBABY MEMORY BOOK

FRIENDS FUR-EVER

SASQUATCH BOOKS
SEATTLE

Printed in China

SASQUATCH BOOKS with colophon is a registered
trademark of Penguin Random House LLC

27 26 25 24 23   9 8 7 6 5 4 3 2 1

Editor: Jen Worick
Production editor: Isabella Hardie
Production designer: Alison Keefe
Cover design by Susanna Ryan and Alison Keefe

ISBN: 978-1-63217-495-6

Sasquatch Books
1325 Fourth Avenue, Suite 1025
Seattle, WA 98101

SasquatchBooks.com

MIX
Paper | Supporting
responsible forestry
FSC® C008047

Contents

Introduction

Dear Dog,

If you're reading this, that means—wait, you can READ?! Wow, we figured you were something special, but this takes matters to a whole new level! It makes perfect sense that your devoted dog parent wanted to record and remember your story, excellent taste in treats, and all the wonderful times you have together to share with your grandpuppies someday (in case the 10,000 photos of you on their phone just won't cut it).

The first two sections of this book are for your human to dish about the journey you've had so far, from how you first joined hearts to your favorite spots to sniff around town. If you two have been besties for a while, your human may be able to answer these prompts right away. If you're a new arrival, it may take a little longer for them to learn all the ins and outs of your deep soul. Either way, it's fine! If a page or prompt isn't making their proverbial tail wag, they can skip it and return another time.

The latter half of the book, beginning with "Day in the Life," is for recording moments and memories as they happen, whether it's great walks, unforgettable road trips, or all the adorable things you do at home. Keeping this book in a visible place will serve as a reminder for your human to add to it over the months and years ahead—you just need to remember NOT to eat, gnaw, chomp, nibble, or otherwise destroy it, okay?

Love,
Dog Days

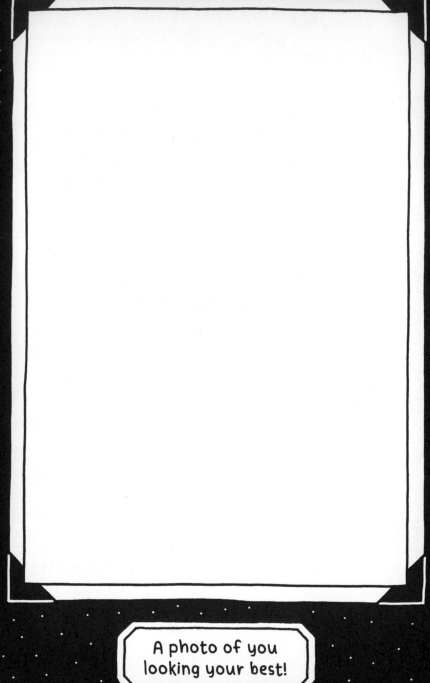

A photo of you
looking your best!

All About You

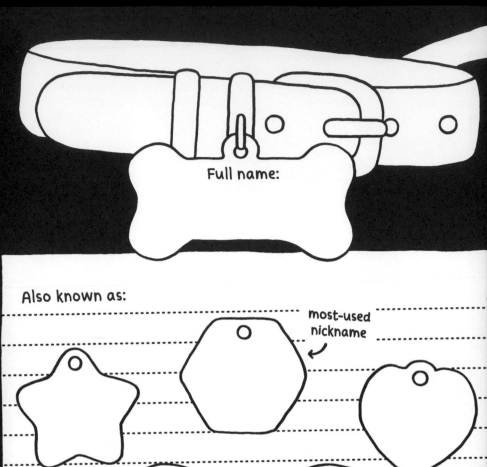

Full name:

Also known as:

most-used
nickname

what I call out at the dog
park when I REALLY want
to get your attention

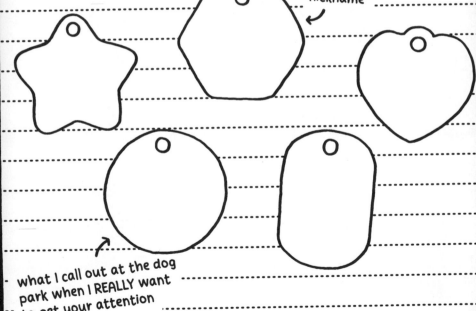

How you got your name:

....

....

....

....

....

....

....

....

Other names I considered:

....

....

....

....

....

....

....

....

....

When someone asks what breed you are, I say:

Eye colors:	Coat colors:

Everyday object similar to your size:

Physical characteristic most likely to melt hearts:

Softest part of you:

Small feature most people wouldn't notice unless they have stared at you as much as I have:

Favorite areas to receive a pet or scratch:

Your stance on belly rubs: ☐ for
☐ against
☐ it's complicated

What I love
about your...

nose:

ears:

eyes:

paws:

"Gotcha" day: _____

Where we met face-to-snout for the first time:

_____

_____

_____

_____

The first thing I noticed about you:

_____

_____

_____

_____

The moment I knew you were the dog for me:

_____

_____

_____

_____

_____

_____

_____

_____

_____

_____

Birth year: ☐ exact ☐ ruff guess

What I know about your life before we met:

☐ your background is mysterious

How I found out about you:

Where we live:

Other people and animals in our household:

☐ it's just the two of us!

Name: _____ Relationship: _____

Species: ☐ dog ☐ human ☐ other: _____

Name: _____ Relationship: _____

Species: ☐ dog ☐ human ☐ other: _____

Name: _____ Relationship: _____

Species: ☐ dog ☐ human ☐ other: _____

Name: _____ Relationship: _____

Species: ☐ dog ☐ human ☐ other: _____

Name: _____ Relationship: _____

Species: ☐ dog ☐ human ☐ other: _____

How I felt about bringing you home:

Memories from our first day together:

Pup Personality Profile

How you rank:

○ ○ ○ ○ ○ ← not so much...

● ● ● ● ● ← ALL THE TIME!

Curious ○ ○ ○ ○ ○

Playful ○ ○ ○ ○ ○

Intelligent ○ ○ ○ ○ ○

Loving ○ ○ ○ ○ ○

Energetic ○ ○ ○ ○ ○

Perceptive ○ ○ ○ ○ ○

Dramatic ○ ○ ○ ○ ○

Outgoing ○ ○ ○ ○ ○

Anxious ○ ○ ○ ○ ○

Independent ○ ○ ○ ○ ○

Personality traits I noticed early on in our relationship:

Three words that describe you:

One word that could NEVER be used to describe you:

Words that make your ears perk up:

Songs that get your tail wagging:

☐ for the record, you do not have a tail (and I love you for it!)

Scents that make your nose go wild:

Things you'll bark at, no matter what:

BARK!
BARK!
BARK!

Five things you LOVE:

Five things you LOATHE:

Dog Days Yearbook

I voted, and the title you'd be most likely to receive is:

☐ Most Athletic

☐ Class Clown

☐ Most Likely to Succeed

☐ Best Hair

☐ Party Animal

☐ Biggest Flirt

☐ Future Actor

☐ Most Likely to Eat
ALL the Toilet Paper

TRUE or FALSE?

You think EVERY package is for you.

☐ TRUE   ☐ FALSE

I trust you with an unattended cookie.

☐ TRUE   ☐ FALSE

Neighborhood squirrels have been known to give you the side-eye.

☐ TRUE   ☐ FALSE

You're ALWAYS on the trail of the hottest new scents in life.

☐ TRUE   ☐ FALSE

Vacuum cleaners are your mortal enemy.

☐ TRUE   ☐ FALSE

You don't worry about making a good first impression.

☐ TRUE   ☐ FALSE

Treats are your love language.

☐ TRUE   ☐ FALSE

You would rather romp in the snow than have fun in the sun.

☐ TRUE   ☐ FALSE

I am confident that you would at least attempt to rescue
a child who fell down a well.

☐ TRUE   ☐ FALSE

You are a beautiful and perfect angel dog, yes you are,
yes you are...

☐ TRUE   ☐ ...E

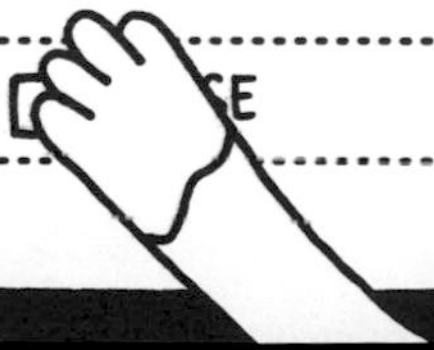

My favorite picture
of us

Our Inner Circle

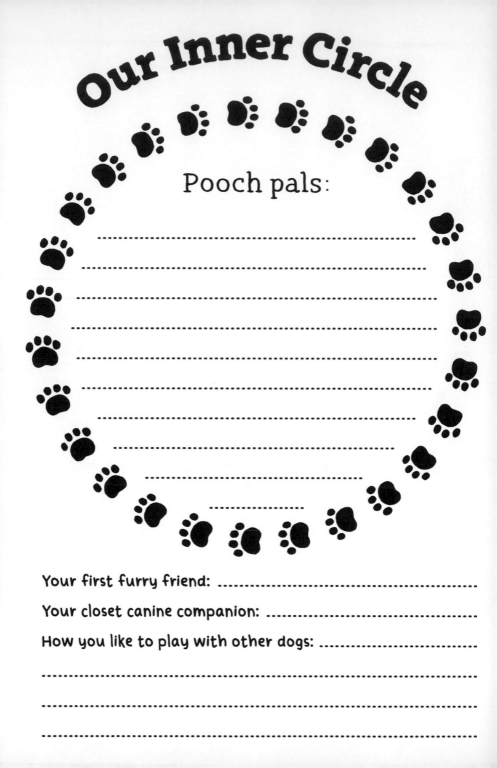

Pooch pals:

....

....

....

....

....

....

....

....

....

Your first furry friend: ....

Your closet canine companion: ....

How you like to play with other dogs: ....

....

....

....

Human friends:

....
....
....
....
....
....
....
....
....

The human friends who have known you the longest: ....
....
The person most likely to dogsit: ....
Your most humanlike behavior: ....
....
....
....
....

Activities we like
to do together
at home:

Ways you keep yourself entertained around the house:

FOOD

Typical daily feeding schedule:

Time of day	Amount	Food type

Foods and flavors you like:	Foods and flavors you dislike:

Bone appétit! I designed a "gotcha" day cake with all your favorite treats and flavors in mind:

Ideas: peanut butter frosting, kibble sprinkles, a dash of pumpkin powder, dental bones, remnants of an old sandwich, decorative spinach, dog-shaped cake topper lovingly formed with cheese

Our Clean Routine

Ways we keep up appearances:

✓	Activity	Frequency	At home or with a pro?
	bathing		
	brushing fur		
	trimming fur		
	trimming nails		
	ear cleaning		
	brushing teeth		

This is what the weird old towel I use on you most often looks like →

Towel's origin story:

....

....

....

Temperature Check

Your ranking on the Grooming Enthusiasm Meter:

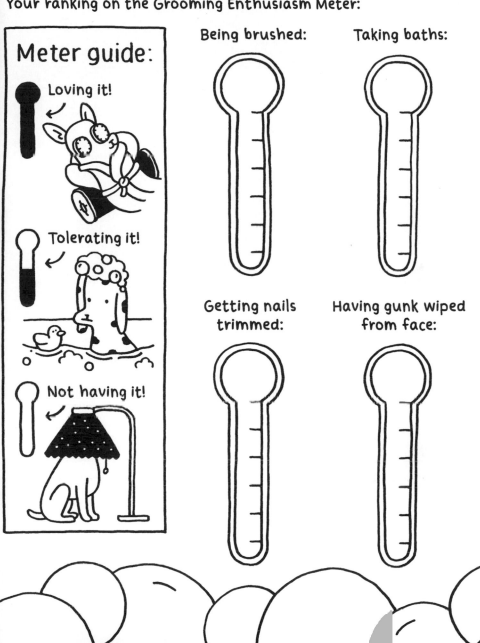

Meter guide:

Loving it!

Tolerating it!

Not having it!

Being brushed:

Taking baths:

Getting nails trimmed:

Having gunk wiped from face:

SLEEP

Favorite spots for an afternoon snooze:

Where you usually sleep at night:

Creature comforts you enjoy cuddling with:

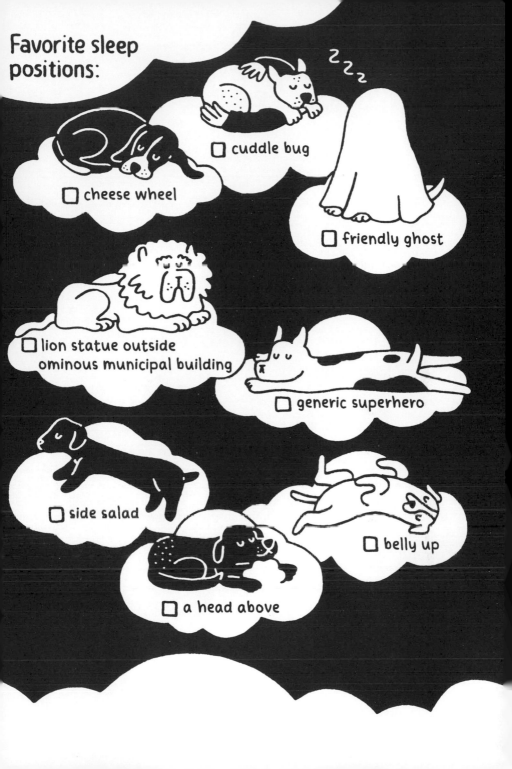

Dog Toy Hall of Fame

Choice chew toy:

Received as a gift:

Lifelong frenemy:

Gone but not forgotten:

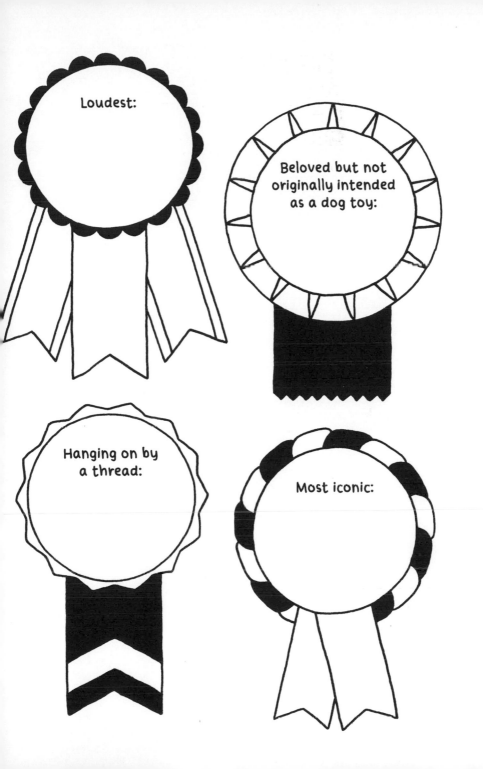

Loudest:

Beloved but not originally intended as a dog toy:

Hanging on by a thread:

Most iconic:

Training

(because being such a good dog is hard work!)

Training, obedience, and socialization classes you've taken:

Year	Class	Location

Ways we work on training and recall together:

....

....

....

The biggest behavioral changes I've observed since knowing you:

....

....

....

....

Hair Raisers!

I drew an arrow to indicate how you respond to these potentially frightful facts of life:

delivery vehicles

thunder

birds
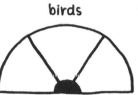

fireworks

leaf blowers

unfamiliar dogs

cats

children's birthday parties

blenders

doorbells

joggers

people wearing socks with sandals

Tricks and commands you know:

....
....
....
....
....
....
....

Spin!

Shake!

....
....
....
....
....
....

....
....
....
....
....
....
....

Roll over!

Tricks and commands I *wish* you knew:

☐ Repot the houseplants you knocked over!

☐ Prepare taxes!

☐ Find the end of a roll of tape!

☐ Fold fitted sheets!

☐ Remember old passwords!

☐ Pretend to be me at work!

Hall of
SHAME

Even the most well-trained pups can wake up on the wrong side of the dog bed. Here are the most scandalous faux *paws* you've ever committed!

Medical Care

Our veterinarian:
....

How you feel about going to the vet:
....
....
....

Bribery methods that are always successful with you:
....
....

Medications you take regularly:
....
....
....

Foods I hide your pills in:
....
....
....

Allergies:
....
....
....

Ongoing medical concerns:
....
....
....

Your Dream Cone!

Trot down the street with dignity AND style with this dream dog cone, designed just *fur* you!

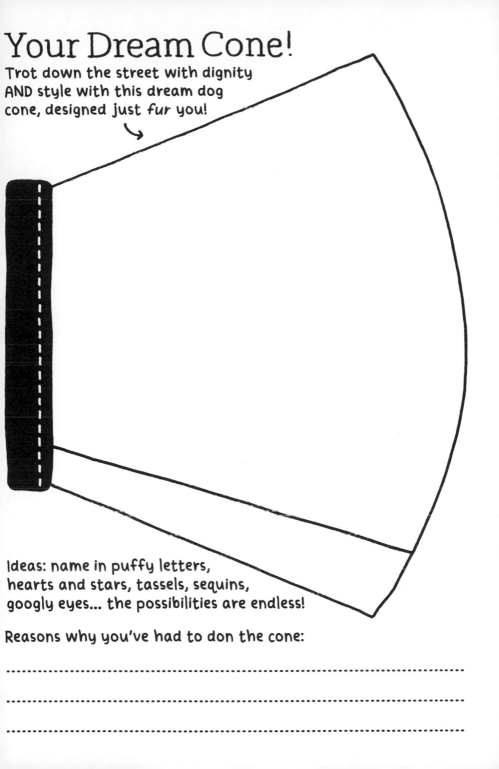

Ideas: name in puffy letters, hearts and stars, tassels, sequins, googly eyes... the possibilities are endless!

Reasons why you've had to don the cone:

....

....

....

Confessions of a Pet parent

Hey, dog—look! Over there! A truck full of old bread just toppled over, and now the street is a carbohydrate free-for-all!

Whew, now that the dog is distracted, I'm ready to spill the tea on all my pet parent secrets.

The most ridiculous thing I've ever done to pamper or spoil you:

....

....

....

....

Songs I serenade you with or special rituals we do when no one else is around:

....

....

....

....

Other dogs I know that I think are very good dogs:

....

....

....

I have said that food is "all gone" when it is not, in fact, all gone.

☐ TRUE   ☐ FALSE

You have your own social media account...

☐ TRUE   ☐ FALSE

...and it has more followers than mine.

☐ TRUE   ☐ FALSE

I give you better medical attention and care than I give myself.

☐ TRUE   ☐ FALSE

If you're sleeping on the couch, I will lie in uncomfortable positions so I don't disturb you.

☐ TRUE   ☐ FALSE

I kiss your paws more often than I would like to admit.

☐ TRUE   ☐ FALSE

You have peed right next to a "no dogs allowed" sign at least once in your life.

☐ TRUE   ☐ FALSE

I have used you as an excuse to cancel plans or leave a social event early...

☐ TRUE   ☐ FALSE

...at least a dozen times.

☐ TRUE   ☐ FALSE

Around the Neighborhood

Parks we like to visit:

Dog-friendly places we frequent:

Businesses with dog treat jars:

Our most-used public
garbage can or
dog waste receptacle:

Favorite neighborhood tree:

Common critters we see:

Street with the most
intriguing scents:

Homes of our pooch pals:

Favorite outdoor activities to do together:

....
....
....
....
....
....
....
....
....

Favorite places for a walk or adventure:

....
....
....
....
....
....
....
....
....
....
....

Top three sidewalk finds you would most likely stop and investigate on a walk:

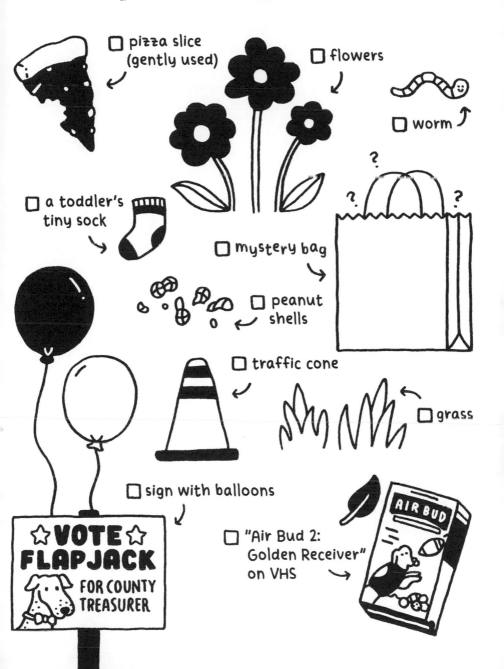

☐ pizza slice (gently used)

☐ flowers

☐ worm

☐ a toddler's tiny sock

☐ mystery bag

☐ peanut shells

☐ traffic cone

☐ grass

☐ sign with balloons

☐ "Air Bud 2: Golden Receiver" on VHS

☆ VOTE ☆ FLAPJACK FOR COUNTY TREASURER

AIR BUD

Dog Park Badges

I would award you the following dog park badges:

☐ The Disc Dynamo!

☐ The Ringleader!

☐ The Escape Artist!

☐ The Stick Sleuth!

☐ The Mud Magnet!

☐ The Ball Bandit!

☐ The Show-Off!

☐ The "I'm Not Here to Make Friends, I'm Here to Eat Grass Alone"!

Holidays and special occasions we celebrate in spring:

....

....

....

....

....

Activities we do together:

....

....

....

....

....

....

Holidays and special occasions we celebrate in summer:

....
....
....
....
....

Activities we do together:

....
....
....
....
....
....

Holidays and special occasions we celebrate in fall:

....

....

....

....

....

Activities we do together:

....

....

....

....

....

....

Holidays and special occasions we celebrate in winter:

....

....

....

....

....

Activities we do together:

....

....

....

....

....

....

What we would do on one perfect day together:

_____
_____
_____
_____
_____
_____
_____
_____
_____
_____

Unexpected ways my life has changed since you arrived:

_____
_____
_____
_____
_____
_____
_____
_____
_____
_____

I didn't know this about you when we first met:

_____
_____
_____
_____
_____
_____
_____
_____
_____
_____
_____
_____
_____
_____
_____
_____
_____
_____
_____
_____
_____
_____
_____

7:30 a.m.
Breakfast

7:31 a.m.
Spit out allergy medicine
I tried to sneak into your breakfast

10:30 a.m.
Midmorning snooze (on couch)

12:00 p.m.
Stared out window wistfully

ZZZ

1:30 p.m.
Early afternoon snooze (on rug)

2:45 p.m.
Walked around neighborhood
(found a slice of cheese
under a bush!)

4:30 p.m.
Tore squeaker out of
stuffed carrot toy

5:00 p.m.
Dinner

FOOD

6:15 p.m.
I brushed your coat

7:30 p.m.
We snuggled on couch and
binge-watched a baking show

Map tips (for human readers):

- 🐾 Take notes throughout the day and add to the pages later.
- 🐾 To maximize your map, try on a day where you'll spend most of the time around your dog.
- 🐾 Need a starting point? Check in on the top of each hour and record what your dog is doing.

Day in the Life

What DO you do all day? To answer that question once and for all, I used words, lines, pictures, and arrows to create a Day in the Life map (like the example on the left!).

Date:

Date:

Date:

Date:

Date:

Date:

Walks to Remember

When paws hit the pavement, there's no telling what magical sights and smells await. These walks were ones for the memory book!

Date: ....

Weather: ☼ ☼ ☁ ☔ ☃

Where we walked: ....
....

We saw: ....
....
....

You sniffed: ....
....
....

I'll never forget this walk because: ....
....
....
....
....
....
....
....
....
....

Date: ....

Weather: ☀ ☀ ☁ 🌧 🌨

Where we walked: ....
....

We saw: ....
....
....

You sniffed: ....
....
....

I'll never forget this walk because: ....
....
....
....
....
....
....
....
....
....

Date: ....

Weather: ☼ ☼ ☁ ☂ ☂

Where we walked: ....

....

We saw: ....

....

....

You sniffed: ....

....

....

I'll never forget this walk because: ....

....

....

....

....

....

....

....

....

....

Date: ....

Weather: ☀ ⛅ ☁ 🌦 🌨

Where we walked: ....
....

We saw: ....
....
....

You sniffed: ....
....
....

I'll never forget this walk because: ....
....
....
....
....
....
....
....
....
....
....

EEK!

Date: ....

Weather: ☀ ☼ ☁ 🌧 🌨

Where we walked: ....
....

We saw: ....
....
....

You sniffed: ....
....
....

I'll never forget this walk because: ....
....
....
....
....
....
....
....
....
....

Date: ....

Weather: ☼ ⛅ ☁ 🌧 🌨

Where we walked: ....
....

We saw: ....
....
....

You sniffed: ....
....
....

I'll never forget this walk because: ....
....
....
....
....
....
....
....
....
....

Date: ....

Weather: ☀ ⛅ ☁ 🌧 🌨

Where we walked: ....

....

We saw: ....

....

....

You sniffed: ....

....

....

I'll never forget this walk because: ....

....

....

....

....

....

....

....

....

....

....

Date: ....

Weather: ☀ ⛅ ☁ 🌧 🌨

Where we walked: ....
....

We saw: ....
....
....

You sniffed: ....
....
....

I'll never forget this walk because: ....
....
....
....
....
....
....
....
....
....
....
....

Date: ....

Weather:  ☀ ⛅ ☁ 🌧 🌨

Where we walked: ....

....

We saw: ....

....

....

You sniffed: ....

....

....

I'll never forget this walk because: ....

....

....

....

....

....

....

....

....

....

Date: ....

Weather:

Where we walked: ....
....

We saw: ....
....
....

You sniffed: ....
....
....

I'll never forget this walk because: ....
....
....
....
....
....
....
....
....
....

Dog Park Diaries

Dachshund drama, Golden Retriever gossip, and other unforgettable *tails* from outings to the dog park!

Date: _____ Dog park: _____

I: ☐ did ☐ did not
   have to make small talk with fellow dog parents
You: ☐ made new friends ☐ made new mortal enemies

Dear Dog Park Diary,

Date: _____ **Dog park:** _____

I: ☐ did ☐ did not
  choose the appropriate footwear
You: ☐ fetched ☐ frolicked ☐ flailed

Dear Dog Park Diary,

....

....

....

....

....

....

....

....

....

....

....

....

....

....

....

....

BOW-WOW!

Date: _____   Dog park: _____

I: ☐ did ☐ did not
remember the dog waste bags
You: ☐ charmed ☐ chased ☐ chomped

Dear Dog Park Diary,

I ♥ GRASS

Date: _____ Dog park: _____

I: ☐ did ☐ did not
 see your doggy doppelgänger
You: ☐ barked (approvingly) ☐ barked (disapprovingly)

Dear Dog Park Diary,

FRIENDS
FUR-EVER

Date: **Dog park:**

I: ☐ did   ☐ did not
    look at my phone to avoid making eye contact with someone
You: ☐ sniffed grass   ☐ sniffed trash   ☐ sniffed another dog

Dear Dog Park Diary,

....

....

....

....

....

....

....

....

....

....

....

....

....

....

....

....

....

....

Date: _____ Dog park: _____

I: ☐ did ☐ did not
  pet someone else's dog
You: ☐ did something sort of embarrassing ☐ made me proud!

Dear Dog Park Diary,
....

....

....

....

....

....

....

....

....

....

....

....

....

....

....

....

....

SO FETCH!

GREETINGS FROM THE CAR WINDOW

AHOY

PAWS-PORT

YAP! YAP! YAP!

FUR-EVER

PUP TENT

On the Road

Dispatches from road trips, overnight stays, and other adventures away from home

Dates:

Destination:

Trip companions:

....

....

Dog highlight:

....

....

....

Human highlight:

....

....

....

Moment with you I hope to always remember:

....

....

....

....

....

Dates:

Destination:

Trip companions:
....
....
....

Dog highlight:
....
....
....

Human highlight:
....
....
....

Moment with you I hope to always remember:
....
....
....
....
....

Dates:

Destination:

BARK
BARK
BARK

Trip companions:
....
....
....
Dog highlight:
....
....
....
....
Human highlight:
....
....
....
....
Moment with you I hope to always remember:
....
....
....
....
....

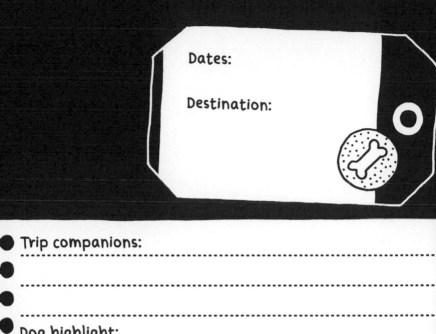

Dates:

Destination:

Trip companions:

....

....

Dog highlight:

....

....

....

Human highlight:

....

....

....

Moment with you I hope to always remember:

....

....

....

....

Dates:

Destination: ⊙

DOG

Trip companions:
....
....

Dog highlight:
....
....
....

Human highlight:
....
....
....

Moment with you I hope to always remember:
....
....
....
....

Dates:

Destination:

Trip companions:

....

....

Dog highlight:

....

....

....

Human highlight:

....

....

....

Moment with you I hope to always remember:

....

....

....

....

....

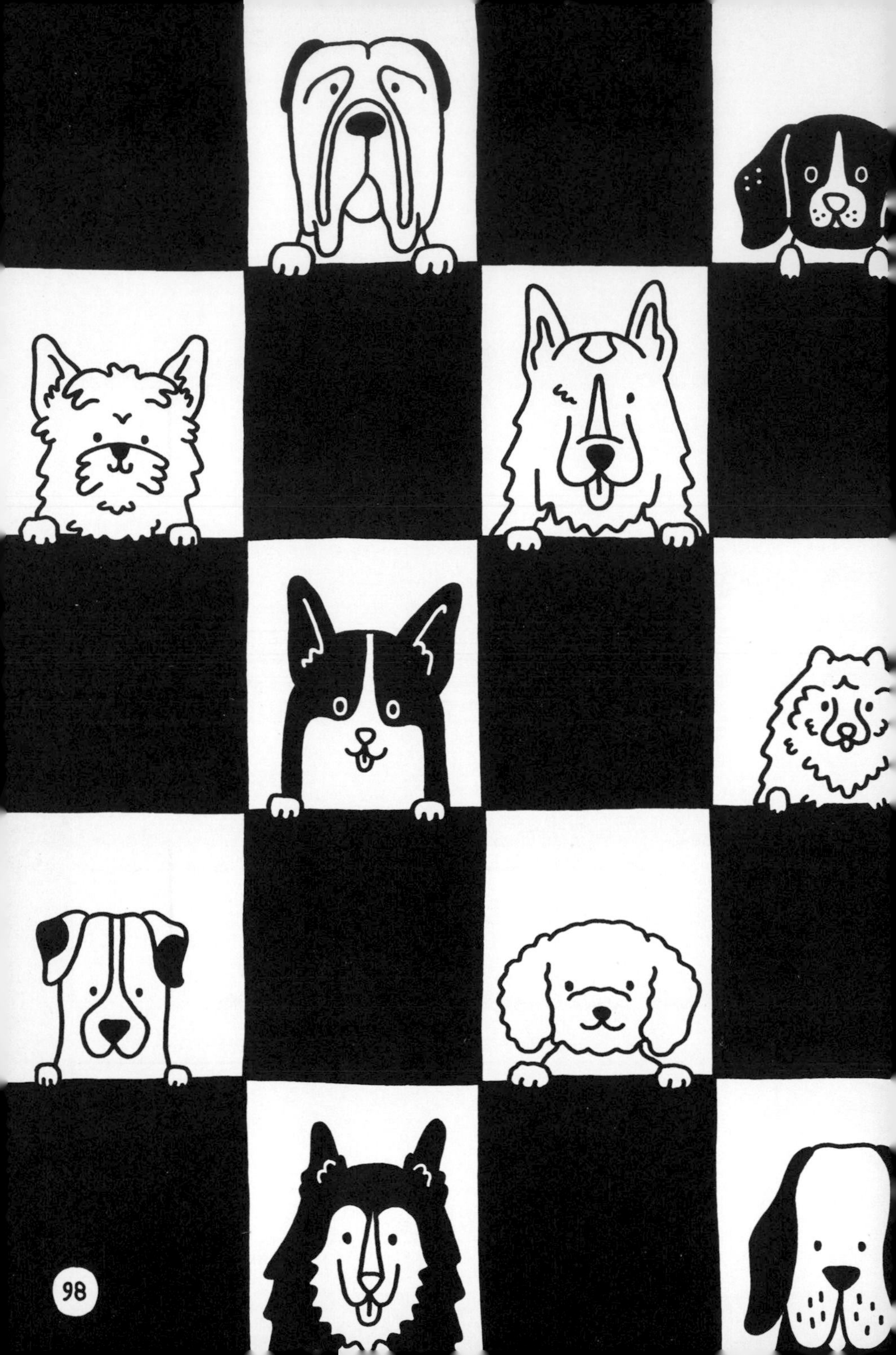

Memorable Moments

Acts that left me thinking,
"I can't believe you just did that!"

That was **smart!**

Date	Event

Date	Event

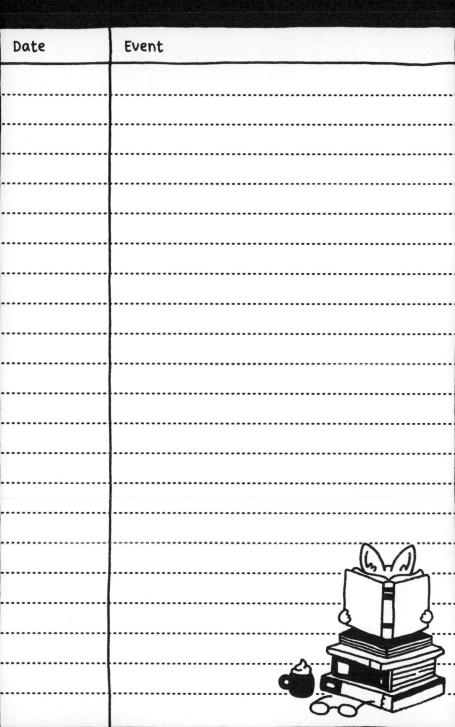

That was **funny!**

Date	Event

Date	Event

That was **cute!**

Date	Event

Date	Event

That was **weird!**

Date	Event

Date	Event

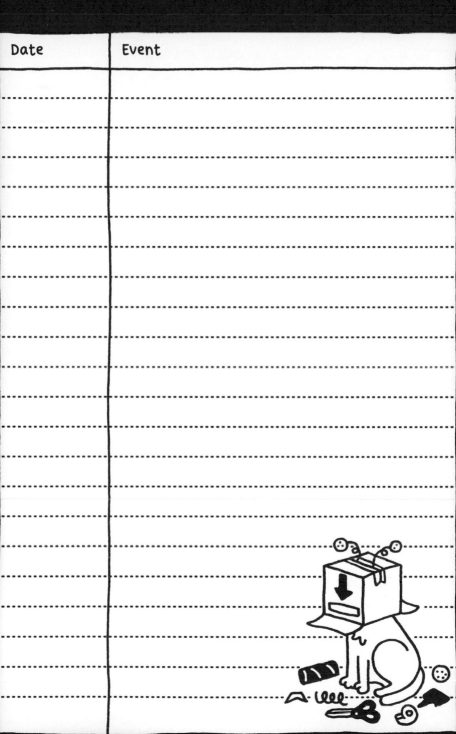

Other moments

Date	Event

Date	Event

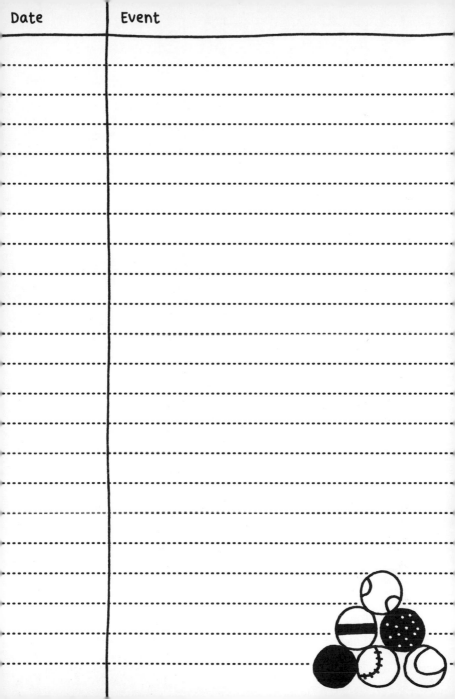

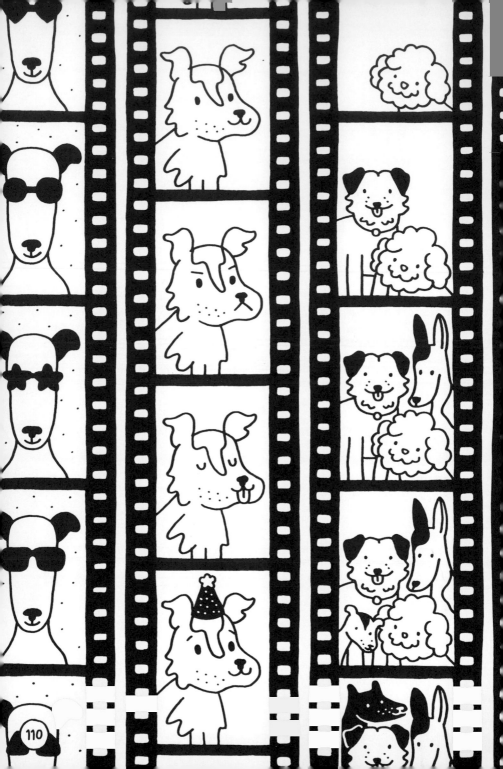

Your Highlight Reel

First times, big moves, small victories, and other life changes

Date	Milestone or significant event

Date	Milestone or significant event

Date	Milestone or significant event

Date	Milestone or significant event

Date	Milestone or significant event

Date	Milestone or significant event

Good Times Together

Photos, drawings, notes, and reflections from all those good times together

Dog Doodle Art Gallery

As if you weren't *already* a gallery-worthy masterpiece, now you're the artistic muse for me and our friends!

My finest
portrait of you

Year:

You, drawn with my eyes closed

Year:

You, drawn without picking up my pen

Year:

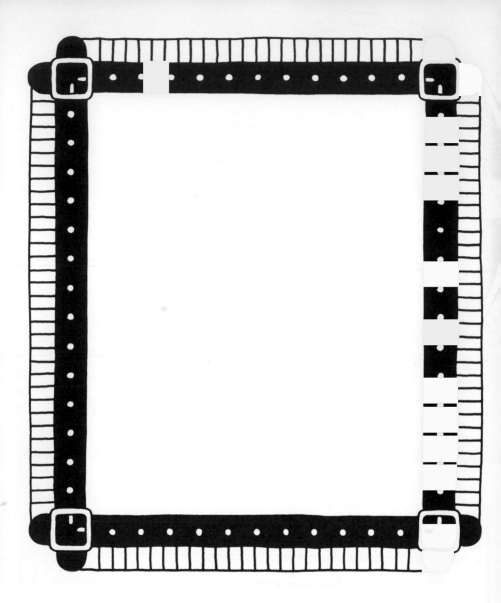

You, drawn by
a friend

Artist:

Year:

You, drawn by
a friend

Artist:

Year:

You, drawn by
a friend

Artist:

Year:

Pawtrait of
you

Year:

Pawtrait of
me

Year:

YOU PUT THE "AW" IN "PAW"!

Puppy Love Letters

Your human friends share
all the things they love
about you!

Friend name: ....

Word I think of when I think of you: ....

Memorable moment with you I will always treasure:

....

....

....

....

My hopes and dreams for you: ....

....

....

....

....

Friend name: ....

Word I think of when I think of you: ....

Memorable moment with you I will always treasure:

....

....

....

....

My hopes and dreams for you: ....

....

....

....

....

Friend name: ....

Word I think of when I think of you: ....

Memorable moment with you I will always treasure:

....

....

....

....

My hopes and dreams for you: ....

....

....

....

....

Friend name: ....

Word I think of when I think of you: ....

Memorable moment with you I will always treasure:

....

....

....

....

My hopes and dreams for you: ....

....

....

....

....

Friend name: ....

Word I think of when I think of you: ....

Memorable moment with you I will always treasure:

....

....

....

....

My hopes and dreams for you: ....

....

....

....

....

....

Friend name: ....

Word I think of when I think of you: ....

Memorable moment with you I will always treasure:

....

....

....

....

My hopes and dreams for you: ....

....

....

....

....

Credits

Your human
lives in   .
When not tending to your
needs,   enjoys

                              ,

                              ,
and   .

Susanna Ryan lives in Seattle. If she could be a dog, she would want to be a scrappy and mysterious mixed breed named Licorice Allsorts.